WITHDRAWN

Amazing Mysteries
UFOs AND ALIENS

Anne Rooney

A⁺
Smart Apple Media

Smart Apple Media
P.O. Box 3263, Mankato, MN 56002

Printed in the United States of America at Corporate Graphics, North Mankato, Minnesota.

            Library of Congress Cataloging-in-Publication Data
Rooney, Anne.
  UFOs and aliens / Anne Rooney.
      p. cm. -- (Amazing mysteries)
  Includes index.
  ISBN 978-1-59920-368-3 (hardcover)
  1. Unidentified flying objects--Juvenile literature. 2. Extraterrestrial beings--Juvenile literature. I. Title.
  TL789.2.R66 2010
  001.942--dc22
                            2008050440

Created by Q2AMedia
Editor: Honor Head
Art Director: Rahul Dhiman
Designers: Harleen Mehta, Shilpi Sarkar
Picture Researchers: Sujatha Menon, Shreya Sharma
Line Artist: Sibi N. Devasia
Coloring Artists: Ajay Luthra, Mahender Kumar, Subash Vohra

Picture credits
t=top b=bottom c=center l=left r=right

Cover Image: Mary Evans Picture Library/ Photolibrary, Inset: Q2AMedia

Insides: Mary Evans Picture Library/ Photolibrary: 5t, Mary Evans Picture Library/ Photolibrary: 8b, Mary Evans Picture Library/
Photolibrary: 9b, CNES/ Associated Press: 10b, Mary Evans Picture Library / Alamy: 11b, Hulton Archive/ Stringer/ Getty Images: 13r,
Jonaspas/ iStockphoto: 14b, Mary Evans Picture Library/ Photolibrary: 15l, Medical-on-Line/ Alamy: 16b, Mary Evans Picture Library/
Photolibrary: 17r, Mary Evans Picture Library/ Photolibrary: 18r, L. Zacharie/ Alamy: 20b, David Zaitz/ Photolibrary: 21m, James
Aylott/ Contributor/ Getty images: 22b, www.alienvideo.net and www. alien-ufo-research.com: 23, Neil McAllister / Alamy: 24b, Joel
Shawn/ Shutterstock: 25m, Nasa: 26m, Ray Nelson/ Photolibrary: 28b, Nasa: 29t.

Q2A Media Art Bank: 4, 6, 7, 12, 19, 27.

DAD0034a
42010

9 8 7 6 5 4 3 2

Contents

Visitors from Space

People have reported seeing strange things in the sky for many hundreds of years—and wondered if life exists on other planets. There are lots of reports and sightings that suggest it might.

We Are Not Alone

There are thousands of millions of stars in the **universe**. Lots of those probably have planets. Surely some must have planets like Earth? If there are **aliens** out there, perhaps we can get in touch with them. Or they might visit us. Maybe they have done so already.

! Some people say they have met aliens from outer space.

Alien Visitors

Many people believe aliens have already been to Earth. They say they have seen alien spaceships. Some even believe they have met aliens, or been taken onto alien spacecraft. Unidentified flying objects—**UFOs**—are strange objects or lights in the sky. People have seen them all over the world for hundreds of years. Could these lights be alien spaceships?

! Strange glowing globes filled the sky over Basel, Switzerland, in 1566. Could they have been alien spacecraft?

MYSTERY MOMENT

In 1953, a taxi driver in Mexico named Salvador Villanueva saw two strange creatures. They were nearly 4 feet (120 cm) tall and wore overalls and wide, shiny belts full of holes. They had metal collars and carried helmets. The aliens spoke with a strange accent. They invited Salvador into their round spaceship, but he was scared and ran away.

Unidentified Flying Objects

Whirling wheels of fire, giant disks, and tubes that fly through the sky: alien spaceships have come in all shapes and sizes.

Night Lights

Far back in history, there are records of people seeing strange lights and shapes in the sky. In ancient times people called them dragons or angels. Sometimes people thought they were lights from heaven or hell. Now some people think they may have been aliens.

AT-A-GLANCE UFOs

- Most UFOs appear as long and thin, or saucer-shaped flying spacecraft.
- UFOs can show up on radar.
- Aircraft pilots have reported chasing UFOs.
- In war, glowing balls of light have been seen following planes.

! A man named James Hooton drew this strange ship based on the one he saw in Arkansas in 1897.

MYSTERY MOMENT

For six months in 1989–1990, lots of triangular UFOs with brilliant, shining lights flew over Belgium. They appeared night after night and thousands of people saw them. They even showed up on **radar**. The air force sent fighter jets to chase the strange craft away, but could not follow them—the spacecraft always shot off at high speed, then mysteriously disappeared off the radar.

Strange Sights

In the 1880s, people started seeing UFOs shaped like cigars. These UFOs were spotted in Europe and the United States. They weren't airships because airships didn't fly until twenty years later, after 1900. Some people claim they met alien astronauts from these ships, and that the aliens spoke a strange language.

! Long, thin ships were seen over 100 years ago.

Over There!

In 1914, a man in Germany saw a glowing, cigar-shaped object in a field near his house. It had lights shining at the windows. He saw four or five short creatures about 4 feet (120 cm) tall, dressed in light clothes, close to the ship. As he went near, they went into the ship and closed the door. The spaceship took off silently, going straight up into space.

Flying Saucers

People still see cigar-shaped UFOs, but **flying saucers** are more common now. Flying saucers look like disks, or saucers, and have been reported since the 1940s. They are usually silver, and often have a dome on the top with windows. Sometimes the aliens can be seen through the windows.

Gray Disk

In 1948, two boys in Minnesota said that a gray disk landed near them. It was 28 inches, (70 cm) across and 12 inches (30 cm) thick. It spun up into the sky and flew off. Later, an **FBI** investigator found a patch of ground 28 inches (70 cm) across that showed signs of being pressed down by something heavy.

Sharing the Sky

As people took to the skies in aircraft, more and more reports of UFOs flooded in. Some pilots say they have seen mysterious craft flash by or follow them. Pilot Kenneth Arnold was astonished to see nine bright, flashing objects whiz past the light aircraft he was flying in 1947. He told a newspaper, "They flew like a saucer would if you skipped it across the water." So the term "flying saucer" was born.

WHAT'S THE PROOF?

- Reports and drawings by people who have seen UFOs.
- Radar traces showing UFOs that can't be explained.
- Photos of objects in the sky that can't be identified.
- Ancient accounts of objects and lights in the sky from long ago.
- Scorch marks or dents on the ground where UFOs may have landed.

UFOs at War

World War II was the first war to have lots of air battles. Fighter pilots from this time report seeing strange lights flying beside or behind their planes, then mysteriously vanishing. Sometimes people on the ground saw the glowing lights, too. Pilots were soon calling them "foo fighters."

EYE WITNESS

During World War II, pilot Hilary Evans described a cluster of disks seen by aircraft crew as they ran a bombing raid in Germany. He said they were "silver-colored, about one inch (2.5 cm) thick and three inches (8 cm) in diameter" and were "gliding down slowly" in a group.

! Foo fighters, or alien ships, followed fighter plancs closely during World War II.

Close Encounters

Aliens don't always stay in their spaceships up in the sky. Some people say they have met aliens, communicated with them, and even boarded their spacecraft.

Close Encounters of the Third Kind

There are four kinds of close encounters with UFOs and aliens:

- **First kind**—seeing an alien spaceship.
- **Second kind**—seeing evidence of a spacecraft, like marks on the ground.
- **Third kind**—meeting an alien.
- **Fourth kind**—being abducted, or taken away, by aliens for a short time.

! A hole said to have been created by a UFO in France, in 1989

AT-A-GLANCE ALIENS

- Some people say they have met aliens whose spaceships have landed on Earth.

- Most governments say spaceships and aliens don't exist.

- People who see UFOs or aliens often claim they are visited by Men in Black (see page 12) who tell them not to talk about it.

Chasing Aliens

When George Adamski went on a picnic with friends in the Mojave Desert, California, in 1952, he wasn't expecting to meet an alien from Venus, but that's what he says happened. The group saw a cigar-shaped object in the sky being chased by **military** aircraft. The spacecraft then dropped a silver disk which landed in the desert.

Alien from Venus

Adamski found the disk and met a creature who used **telepathy** to tell Adamski he came from Venus and that aliens on Venus were worried about **radiation** from Earth. Adamski said he met the aliens again and they took him to the moon in their spaceship.

WHAT'S THE PROOF?

- Adamski's friends watched his meeting through binoculars. They signed statements agreeing with what he said.
- Adamski saw millions of tiny lights, like fireflies, on his way to the moon. Later, Apollo astronauts saw the same lights.
- No one could identify the object in the photos Adamski took.

! George Adamski had taken photos of UFOs before he met an alien.

No Aliens—That's Official

Governments usually say there are no such things as aliens and UFOs. But is this what they really think? Could it be that governments don't want to admit to the general public that there are aliens in case it causes people to panic? Maybe some governments have proof that aliens exist but won't admit it.

EYE WITNESS

In 1926, young Henry Thomson went outside to play with his friends—and found three aliens in space suits. "Standing peering into the house, were three figures— and they did not look human," he claims. He said they had owl-like faces with large eyes and slit mouths.

Men in Black

People who have had contact with aliens or UFOs are sometimes visited by mysterious men dressed in black. They usually come in groups of three, and take away all evidence, such as photos and videos the alien-spotters might have. The Men in Black tell people not to discuss the aliens or UFOs they saw. They even threaten to hurt people if they talk too much.

! Men in Black— government officials or aliens in disguise?

Strange Visitor

In 1965, Rex Heflin took photos of a UFO from his car in California. Later, he was visited by a man in black who demanded the photo. He said he was from the North American Air Defense Command (NORAD), but NORAD said they had never sent anyone to see Heflin. No one ever found out who the man was.

Government Cover-Up— or Aliens?

Who are the Men in Black? Some people think they work for the U.S. government. Other people say they are aliens in disguise. The Men in Black usually wear dark glasses. Some people have claimed to have seen glowing eyes behind the shades.

! In 1952, British Prime Minister Winston Churchill demanded an investigation into UFOs. No one knows what the final report says.

MYSTERY MOMENT

Do aliens wear socks? A family who had seen a UFO were visited by a strange man. They said he was "almost 7 feet (213 cm) tall, with a small head, dead white skin, enormous frame, but pipe-stem limbs." The man wore socks—and had a wire running up his leg and going into the skin just above his sock.

13

Know Your Aliens!

Would you know an alien if you saw one? People who say they've seen aliens usually describe one of three types—so look out for these! Perhaps you've seen one already.

AT-A-GLANCE ALIENS

Most people who've seen aliens describe one of three types:

- Grays are short, with thin bodies, big heads, and bulging eyes.
- Little green men are green, short, and have big heads.
- Reptilians have slit mouths and scaly skin.

Grays

The classic alien, **grays** are reported more than any other type. They're shorter than humans, with a large head, no hair, big eyes, and pale or greyish skin. Grays are reported most often in the United States.

! A gray is easy to spot —look at that big head!

Space Lizards

Some aliens look like reptiles. Police Officer Herbert Schirmer met **reptilian** aliens in 1967—he said they were about 5 feet (1.5 m) tall, with a long, thin head. Their skin was pale gray and they had a flat nose, slanted eyes, and a slit-like mouth that never moved. They wore tight silver suits, gloves, and boots.

THE WORLD'S MYSTERIES EXPLORED

FATE

JANUARY 1978 75¢

DEATH BY
HELL'S FIRE

CLOSE ENCOUNTERS OF THE THIRD KIND

REPORT A UFO AT YOUR OWN RISK

. . .Plus Many Other Intriguing Features

A man who saw grays described them as "shorter than five feet (1.5 m), and they had bald heads, no hair. Their heads were domed, very large. They looked like **fetuses** *. . .They had large eyes—enormous eyes—almost all brown, without much white in them. The creepiest thing about them were those eyes . . . they just stared through me."*

Little Green Men

Most aliens are gray or pale. Even reptilian aliens are not normally green. But in 1947, a man in Italy saw two green aliens. He says the short creatures had large heads and hands with eight fingers.

! Stories of alien sightings provided a popular subject for magazines.

MYSTERY MOMENT

In 1954, Jessie Roestenberg hid under the table with her children as a large aluminum disk hovered above their house in England. She saw two aliens with white skin. They had very high foreheads and pale hair down to their shoulders.

Alien Abduction

Seeing an alien can be scary—but how about being taken by aliens into their spaceship? Lots of people say it has happened to them—and it doesn't sound very pleasant.

Lost Time

The first thing someone **abducted** by aliens may notice is that they have "lost" time. There is a gap when they can't say where they were. Then they might find strange injuries on their bodies, and have scary dreams. Many people don't remember their abduction for weeks. Suddenly, they recall being in a room with aliens, being questioned, and often having a medical examination.

AT-A-GLANCE ALIENS

- Many people say they have been abducted by aliens.
- They all can't remember what happened immediately, but remember later.
- Many say they were strapped to a table and examined by aliens.
- Some have injuries or other marks made by the aliens.

! Burns and small puncture wounds are often reported by people who say they have been abducted.

Snatched from a Car

In 1961, Betty and Barney Hill were driving along Route 3 in New Hampshire, on their way back from a vacation in Canada. They claim they were both abducted from their car by creatures that Barney saw on the deck of a spacecraft that flew toward them. They saw the lights of the spaceship, then blacked out. Betty and Barney found themselves driving again two hours later. They didn't know what had happened. Later, both had strange dreams. Under **hypnosis**, they told similar stories of aliens examining them.

! Betty Hill describes being abducted by aliens.

WHAT'S THE PROOF?

- 🛸 Reports from people who say they have been taken to alien spaceships.
- 🛸 All abductees describe the same things happening to them.
- 🛸 Some abductees have strange injuries—cuts, burns or other odd marks on their bodies.
- 🛸 A few people have seen someone being abducted.

Alien Scientists

Why do aliens want to abduct us? Perhaps they want to experiment on us. Many abductees claim they were examined by the aliens. Perhaps aliens want to make babies that are half-human and half-alien. Sometimes aliens show people the future of the Earth on a screen. They show scenes of disaster and destruction—maybe they want to warn us.

EYE WITNESS

Travis Walton was abducted in 1975 in front of his friends! They saw a beam of light from a spaceship strike Walton. One said he "rose a foot (0.3 meters) into the air, his arms and legs outstretched, and shot back some 10 feet (3 meters) all the while caught in the glow of the light. His right shoulder hit the earth, and his body sprawled limply over the ground." The men drove away, then came back. There was no sign of Walton. He turned up four days later.

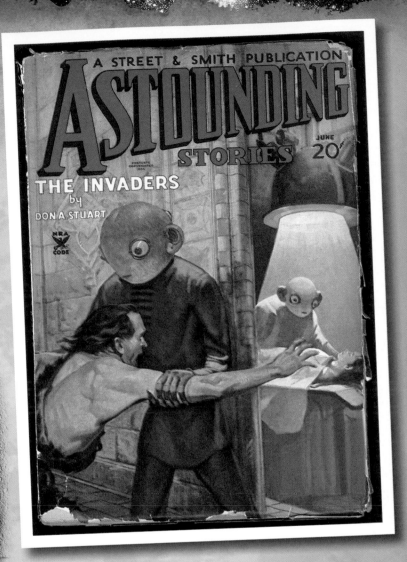

! Stories of alien abduction became common and were featured in popular magazines.

Are We Aliens?

A few people have suggested that the human race is the result of an alien experiment. They say aliens came to Earth millions of years ago and started breeding experiments, or even came to live here. We might all be the result of alien experiments. Will they come back to check on their experiment?

18

MYSTERY MOMENT

In 1976, four men went canoeing near Allagash, Maine. A brightly-lit spacecraft flew over them and they were abducted from their boat for several hours. Twelve years later, all four started to dream of horrible bug-eyed creatures examining their bodies.

The Aliens Have Landed

With all those alien spaceships whizzing around, it would be surprising if they never crashed. Well, maybe they have! Some people think there are a few UFOs hidden around the world.

The Roswell Crash

Many people believe a UFO crashed near Roswell, New Mexico. They said the ship and the alien crew were kept in an aircraft **hangar** in a top-secret location called Area 51. In 1947, the U.S. Air Force said they had found a crashed flying disk near Roswell, then denied it.

! A film that claimed to show a dead alien being examined fooled people for many years. The filmmaker says some shots were real, but not the whole film.

AT-A-GLANCE ALIENS

- A few UFOs may have crashed into Earth.
- Governments may have hidden the wreckage from alien crash landings.
- Some people claim films of crashed UFOs and conversations with aliens are being kept secret by governments.

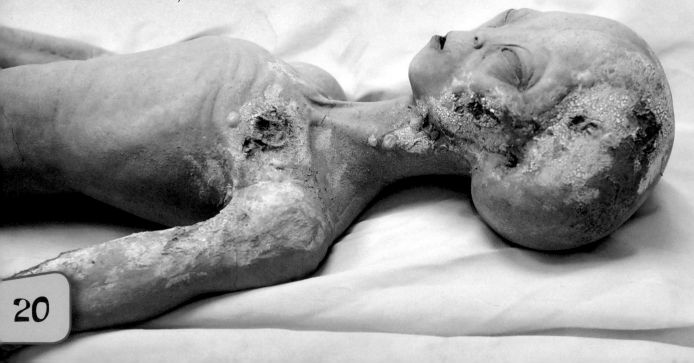

Cover-Up?

Nearly 30 years later, a man involved in recovering the wreckage said there had been a cover-up. More people came forward, saying there were other crashed spaceships and that dead aliens had been examined. This has always been denied by the U.S. government.

Aliens on Film

In 1995, Ray Santilli announced that he had uncovered secret military footage of an alien autopsy at Roswell while doing research for a film. The footage was broadcast across the world. The debate still continues whether the footage was real or not.

UFO CRASH SITE

UFO Museum - 114 N. Main - Roswell

! Did a UFO really crash at Roswell?

MYSTERY MOMENT

Frank Kaufmann says he helped clear up the crashed UFO at Roswell. He saw a spaceship split open, with three alien bodies inside. Another dead alien hung from the spacecraft; a fifth was thrown against a wall. He said they were dressed in silvery, "very, very close-fitting one-piece" clothing that looked "like wet suits." They had small noses, ears and eyes, no hair, and pale, gray skin.

EYE WITNESS

Walter Haut worked at Roswell. He left a statement for after his death. He said: ". . . from a distance, I was able to see a couple of bodies under a canvas tarpaulin. Only the heads extended beyond the covering, and I was not able to make out any features. The heads did appear larger than normal and the contour of the canvas over the bodies suggested the size of a 10-year-old child . . . I am convinced that what I personally observed was some type of craft and its crew from outer space."

Top Secret

Area 51 is so secret that it is not shown on maps. In the past it has been removed from some **satellite pictures** of the Earth. It is used for top-secret military research—it would be a perfect place to hide alien spaceships or even living aliens. Some people think scientists examine UFOs at Area 51 to find out how they work and make similar aircraft. They may also experiment with weapons copied from crashed or captured alien spaceships.

! This top-secret base is in Nevada. Could this be Area 51 where captured aliens and spaceships are hidden?

Russian UFO Crash?

Roswell isn't the only place with a secret alien crash. Another UFO may have crashed in a remote part of Russia in 1969. A film shows Russian soldiers examining a flying saucer partly buried in the ground. The film was smuggled out of Russia. The Russian authorities have said there was no UFO.

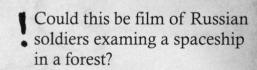
Could this be film of Russian soldiers examing a spaceship in a forest?

WHAT'S THE PROOF?

- A film of an interview with a living alien.
- Bits of spaceship from the crash site.
- Reports of people who saw the crashed spaceship.
- Reports from people who saw aliens at Roswell.

Ancient Visitors

All around the world, there are very old pictures and objects that show figures like aliens and spaceships. Is this proof that aliens have been watching us for thousands of years?

Can You Believe It?

Did alien astronauts come to Earth many thousands of years ago? Some people think they did, and that old descriptions of gods who fly through the sky are really accounts of aliens in spacecraft. They suggest that ancient structures like the pyramids would be too hard to make with very simple tools—so perhaps aliens helped make them.

Alien Art

Caves in South America have pictures that could show spaceships and alien astronauts. A carving on an old temple in Mexico shows something like a spaceman sitting in a rocket, with fire coming out of the bottom. Rock carvings in the desert at Toro Muerto, Peru, seem to show alien astronauts and spaceships. They may be 1,000 years old.

AT-A-GLANCE ALIENS

- There are lots of very old carvings and pictures that could show aliens or spaceships.
- Some people think aliens must have helped to make ancient structures like the pyramids.
- Aliens might be behind some stories of gods or flying magical creatures.

! Does this carving on volcanic rock in Toro Muerto, Peru, show an ancient alien astronaut's space map?

Huge Pictures

On a plain at Nazca, Peru, huge pictures and shapes have been drawn in the ground. Some of the pictures show animals and birds. They are so big they can only be seen properly from the air. The pictures were created hundreds of years ago. Some people think they were made to please alien visitors arriving from space.

! A figure at Nazca as seen from the air. Was it made to greet an alien spaceship?

MYSTERY MOMENT

The Dogon is a tribe in Africa. They have stories about a star system we call Sirius. Their stories tell of three stars. For a long time, scientists thought Sirius had only two stars. But in the 1990s, they discovered an invisible third star. The Dogons say fish-like spirits brought them knowledge of the third star many years ago. Did aliens visit the Dogon and tell them about their star system?

! Has the moon been used as a stopping-station by aliens in the past?

Moon Stop . . .

Could aliens have landed on the moon many years ago? Maybe they used it as a landing strip on trips to look at Earth. Some people believe there is a tower on the moon 1.5 miles (2.4 km) tall. They call it the Shard. They believe there are obelisks—artificial columns—148 feet (45 m) tall on the moon, and a "runway" lined with rows of identical stones.

. . . or Moon-Ship

Some people even think the moon is hollow, and may be a vast spaceship brought here long ago. Old Greek texts talk about a time before the moon was above the Earth, and describe flashes of light coming from it. Could the moon be a spaceship?

Ancient UFO Crash

The mountains between China and Tibet are a vast, empty place where few people go. In 1938, explorers in the mountains found very odd skeletons in a cave. The skeletons had strange, spindly bodies and huge heads. Local people have stories about small, scrawny people with yellow faces and bulging eyes who "came from the clouds, long, long ago."

Story from the Skies?

The explorers also found hundreds of stone disks with strange marks cut in them like a music record. It seems they tell of an alien race called the Dropas whose spacecraft crashed 12,000 years ago. A translation from one disk says: "The Dropas came down from the clouds in their aircraft. Our men, women, and children hid in the caves ten times before sunrise. When at last they understood the sign language of the Dropas, they realized that the newcomers had peaceful intentions."

! There are 716 of these Dropas stone disks, found in a cave in China.

WHAT'S THE PROOF?

- Carvings that seem to show spaceships or aliens.
- Paintings in caves of figures wearing space helmets.
- Pictures drawn on the ground that can only be seen from far above.
- Amazing feats of engineering —like the pyramids—that some people think prove aliens helped ancient people.

Looking for Aliens

The best way to find something is to look for it. The space agency NASA is trying to find aliens by sending messages and spaceships into space.

Listening to Space

The Search for **Extra-Terrestrial** Intelligence—or SETI—is an attempt to find evidence of intelligent aliens in space. It's a huge project that looks at all the **radio waves** coming to Earth from space to find patterns that might be a message. The trouble is, no one speaks alien languages, so they don't know what to look for!

! Radio telescopes scan the skies for signals from outer space.

AT-A-GLANCE ALIENS

- Scientists have sent messages into space, hoping to contact aliens.
- Aliens might be sending us messages.
- Are aliens friendly or dangerous?

Calling All Aliens

As well as waiting for aliens to get in touch with us, NASA has sent out a message that aliens might pick up. The **Arecibo** message was beamed into space in 1974. It was aimed at a cluster of stars 25,000 light years away—which means it will take 25,000 years to get there and another 25,000 years for an answer to get back!

Language!

The NASA *Voyager* spacecrafts set off on an unending voyage into outer space in 1977. On board, each carried a gold disk with recordings of sounds from Earth including a message in 55 languages. One of the languages has not been spoken for 6,000 years—but if aliens really visited Earth thousands of years ago, they might understand it.

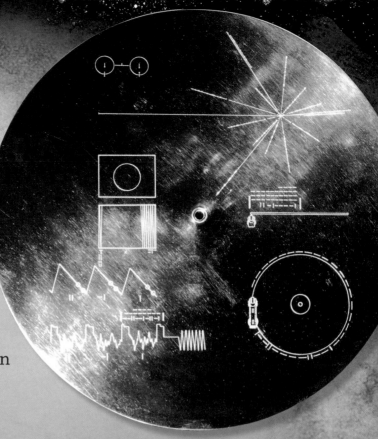

! The gold disk sent into space on a *Voyager* spaceship

How to Get Here

As well as sounds, the disks have pictures showing people and the position of Earth in space. Some people think that was unwise—aliens might follow the directions and come to take over Earth.

MYSTERY MOMENT

Some people believe all life on Earth started with **microbes** from space. In an experiment in 2007, scientists showed that microbes—tiny living things —could survive a trip through space. A **meteorite** could get to Earth from Mars in about a year—so life on Earth could have begun on Mars!

Glossary

abducted	kidnapped and taken away
abductee	someone who has been abducted
aliens	creatures from space
Arecibo	a very sensitive radio telescope in Puerto Rico
autopsy	examination of a dead body to find out why the person or creature died
extra-terrestrial	something that comes from outside Earth, somewhere in space
FBI	Federal Bureau of Investigation, the body that investigates crimes
flying saucer	disk-shaped UFO
fetus	a baby that is still growing inside its mother
grays	aliens with gray skin, a large head, bulging eyes, and a short, skinny body
hangar	large building where aircraft is kept
hypnosis	process of putting someone in a trancelike state to make suggestions to them or ask them questions
meteorite	rocklike object that falls from space to Earth
microbe	very tiny living thing that can only be seen with a microscope
NASA	National Aeronautics and Space Administration. NASA is responsible for space exploration
radar	system that uses radio waves bounced off objects to show where they are and how they are moving

radiation	energy, such as light rays and sound waves, that radiates or comes from a source
radio telescope	telescope that picks up radio waves coming from space
radio waves	radio signals that travel through space and air
reptilians	aliens that are like reptiles, with scaly skin and a slit-like mouth
satellite pictures	photographs of Earth and other planets made by satellites (man-made spacecraft)
telepathy	means of communicating just by thought
UFO	Unidentified Flying Object
universe	all that exists; the whole of space

Index

Web Finder

http://www.alienvideo.net/russian-ufo-crash-video.php
Film footage from the KGB of an investigation of an alien spaceship that crashed in farmland in Russia in 1969

http://www.nasa.gov
Find information on Voyager and other space missions

http://www.eyepod.org/Video-Alien-Interview.html
The alien interview video